sounds and pictures
BOOK 5

by MERVYN BENFORD
illustrated by GERALD WITCOMB

Ladybird Books Ltd Loughborough 1976

um

umbrella

more words to say
under, uncle, ugly

possible initial consonants. Book 6 deals with the double initial consonant, as *'br'* in *bridge*. Some of these can be 'built' from the sounds of the two letters, but it is far better for children to learn them as one combined sound. Often, sounds such as 'sh' in *ship* and 'ch' in *chop,* cannot be built anyway. The initial consonants plus vowel often represent the first vital syllable in any word.

The books show one main word, with its full-colour illustration, together with clues to additional words, in line only, at the foot of the page. Extra words using the same sounds are given for reference and conversation. Parents and teachers should emphasise the combined effect of consonant and vowel, making possible the reading of the whole first syllable. This will prove a great aid to children tackling new words in later reading. If the illustration does not provide sufficient clue, the full starting sound of consonant plus vowel should be given.

Recognising individual letters is essential if the full value of phonic training is to be obtained, so it is important for children to *write* the letters at the same time as learning to say them. Writing practice reinforces memory, a vital part of a child's learning process.

This umbrella is – – .

bu

bus

more words to say
bun, bunch, bundle, buzz, bump,
bucket, but

Can you name these?

bu

butcher

more words to say
bully, bullet, bulldog

The – – – – might eat the – – – – .

cu

cub

more words to say
curry, custard, cut, cuddle

What are these ?

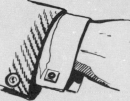

cu

cushions

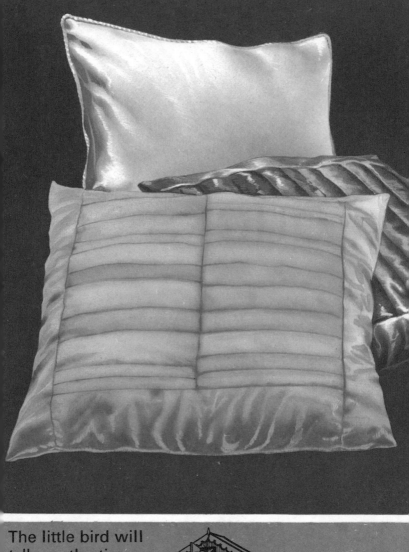

The little bird will
tell you the time.

du

ducks

more words to say
dull, dumb, dusk

This is a rubbish

_ _ _ _ .

What are these ?

fu

funnel

more words to say
fun, fuss, fudge, funny

The proper name for
this is f –––––– .

gu

gulls

more words to say
gum, gully, gulp

What are these?

hu

hut

more words to say
hungry, hum, hull, hurry

You can keep a rabbit
in this ————— .

ju

jumbo jet

more words to say
junk, just, jungle

What are these?

lu

lumberjack

more words to say
lug, lung, lunch

You get this if you
knock yourself

but a prize
from this
if you are
_ _ _ _ _ .

mu

mushrooms

more words to say
muddle, must, mummy

What is this . . . and these?

nu

nuts

more words to say
nun, numb, nuzzle

These are all

- - - - - - - . **358**

pu

puppet

more words to say
pub, pulse, puncture, puff

What are these?

pu

pulley

more words to say
put, puss, pullover

This man will ————, and this man will ————.

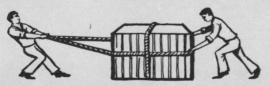

ru

runners

more words to say
run, rub, rustle, rush, rubbish

Clean your paper with this  and your shoes on this.

su

sun

more words to say
such, Sunday, sulk, suck, sudden

Can you do this ---

```
  12      20
+ 14     -10
----     ----
  26      10
```

before you have your ------?

tu

tug

more words to say
tub, tumble, tuck, tuft

vu

vulture

un

uniform

more words to say
use, useful, usually

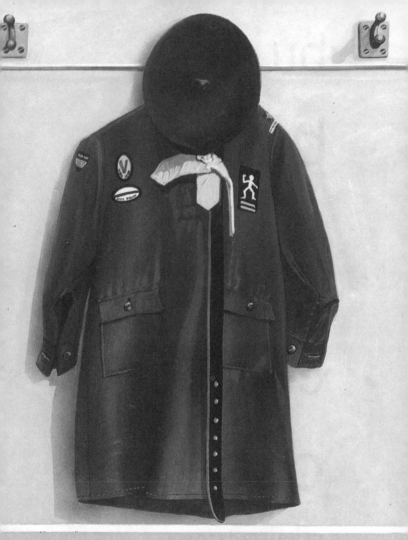

When we add
we use tens
and ─────.

	Tens	**Units**
add	4	6
	2	3
	6	9

bu

bugle

cu

cube

more words to say
cure, curious, cue

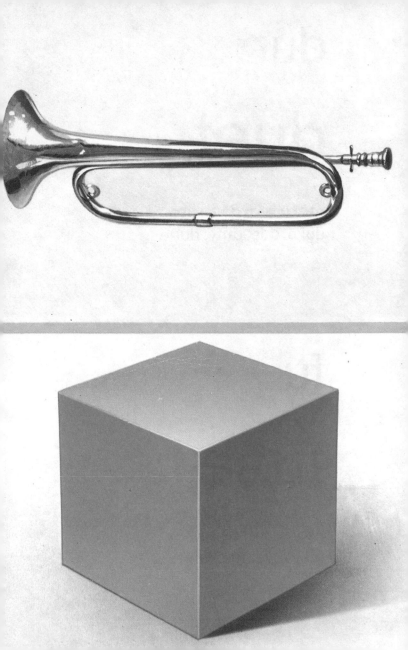

du

duet

more words to say
duke, due, duty, dune

fu

fuse

more words to say
fuel, fuselage, fumes

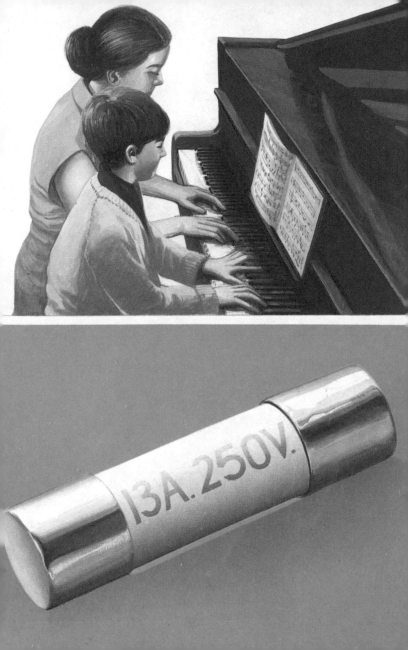

ju

judo

more words to say
junior, jury, Jupiter

Do you know
these months . . .

June July

and what
we get
when we
squeeze a
lemon?

lu

lunar module

more words to say
lute, lupin, Ludo

mu

music

more words to say
mule, mute, mutilate

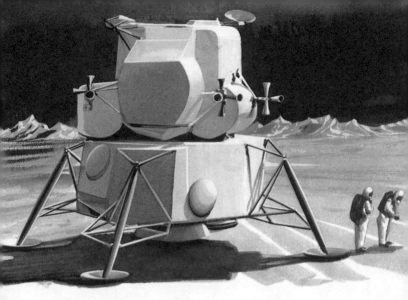

ru

ruler

more words to say
ruin, Ruth, ruthless

tu

tuba

more words to say
tube, tune, tunic

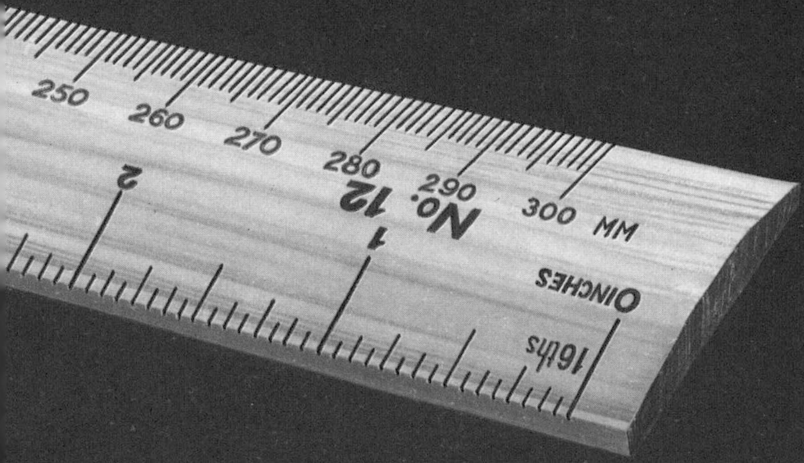
250
260
270
280
290
300 MM
No. 12
2
1
INCHES
16ths

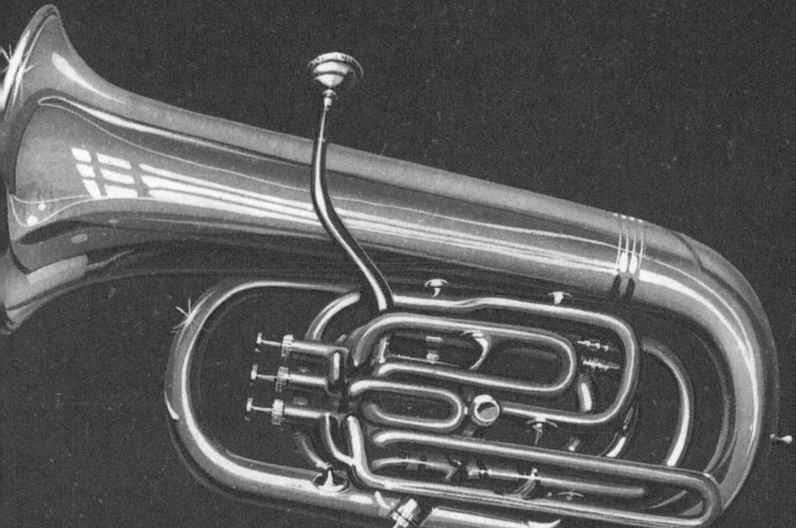

These are in this book—
can you say their names?